Uniquia Manigault

LIVING

IN

TRUTH

Poetry Book
"Volume II The Rebirth"

Poetry that speaks truth, creates healing
and gives therapy to the MIND, BODY & SOUL....

PUBLISHING CO.

Black Girl Beauty

WWW.BLACKGIRLBEAUTYINC.COM

I am unique

WARNING - DISCLAIMER

This book is a work of nonfiction. The purpose of this book is to bring awareness through poetry to things in life that's needed on your path to growth. We have all experienced things that make us happy and unhappy... The question is what will you do with it? Will you allow your story to cripple you? Or will you allow your story to make you great? We all are made perfectly in God's eyesight. As we go through adolescence to adulthood there are things in life, we must learn regardless to how we learn... We must let go of the excuses and understand that everybody has a story and a circumstance whether it is good or bad. LIVING IN TRUTH Volume II The Rebirth will help you understand that no matter what your story is all you have to do is pick your head up with confidence, embrace your true beauty and live your best life UNAPOLOGETICALLY! The author is a very creative writer, who wrote these poems based off of her personal experiences, relationships, trials, tribulations and thirty-one years of life. She expresses herself through poetry. She also challenges you to start journaling TODAY! This information should be used to inspire, cause change, inform and unite. The author shall have neither liability nor responsibility to any person or entity with respect to any loss or damage caused, or alleged to have been caused, directly or indirectly, by the information contained in this book.

"Scriptures written are taken from the King James Version of the Bible.
PUBLISHER: Black Girl Beauty Publishing Co.
(https://www.blackgirlbeautyinc.com)"
ISBN 978-0-9847807-0-9

I would like to dedicate LIVING IN TRUTH Volume II , The Rebirth to those I love that I will never see again on this side... I cried these words to each of you. I miss and love you all. I wear purple for you, every day. I want the world to know you forever. That is my goal and promise to you!

-Wilbert Manigault
-Betty Willaims
-Daijah Manigault
-Tronda "Michelle" Dibble
-Aneesah Washington
-Milton Manigault

ACKNOWLEDGEMENTS AND THANKS

I would like to take the time to first give honor to God for all my many blessings. I'd be nowhere if it weren't for his grace. I'd also like to thank everyone that has assisted and supported me through this long amazing journey. It has not been easy but I am so thankful for every person that has been in my corner pushing me and encouraging me to stay focused on my future. I must thank my mom Amanda Manigault, on every day you are my rock and I thank God for you daily. You've always been there helping me through life and this writing process, I can't thank you enough. And to my father I thank you for showing me a love I could only dream and helping me reach goals I never knew I wanted, I don't know where I'd be without you. There are so many people that have had a major influence in my life and taught me more than I could ever thank them for. I thank you all. I would not have made it to where I am without you all! I love you.

- Uniquia Manigault

Introduction

Living in Truth Vol: II The Rebirth is a collection of poems that take you on a journey through the mind of a person going through a rebirth. Each poem touches on a different thought or experience a person may encounter when trying to change for the better. This book is an awesome tool of motivation for a person on a journey of growth and understanding. L.I.T. V2 The Rebirth is broken down into 6 sections, each section is molded by a scripture from the story of Joseph. The scripture should be used as a reference when experiencing the feelings that are expressed in the section outlined in the table of contents. The poems in the section are the authors intrepretation and understanding to where Joseph was on his journey and how he was able to continue through his similar trials and tribulations. Gaining understanding of Joseph's story will help any and every one traveling through a rebirth. Buckle your seatbelts and get ready you're in for a ride.

Table of Contents

Read: Genesis 42-44

Section III

Read: Genesis 45-46:27

Section IV

When you begin to move toward you purpose life will test you,
remember who you are, remember how far you've, the plans and
changes you've made for you and stay the course

Read: Genesis 46:28-47:28

Section V

There are many levels to the rebirth, it's important we do not get too comfortable change does not happen overnight faith and consistency is key that's how you continue to elevate when life may seem as though you shouldn't

Read: Genesis 47:29-50

Section VI

Acceptance may be one of the hardest steps to walk. Having to be ok with things you cannot change or truths you never wanted to live is HARD. But that's life, that's the main fact they never mention about the rebirth

Read: Genesis 47:29-50

Read: Genesis 37

<u>Section One</u>

The thing about a rebirth is, in the beginning more than likely you won't realize its beginning. You'll just be living life... freely, comfortably, unapologetically and boom something happens everything crashes and then there you are trying to figure things out.

Welcome to the Pluumtree, its open mic night. Here at the Pluumtree feelings are shared freely, stories are revealed truthfully, lessons are given with therapy, words are spoken with honesty. Here we heal our souls through poetry.

Living in Truth Vol 2: The Rebirth was truly a journey. It matured me, introduced me to adulthood showed me some of the things I needed to prepare. And you know what I realized being an adult is hard... ain't it? I mean adulting is truly one hell of an experience, and it never stops. Last year was crazy for me. During all the chaos I went on a whole emotional roller coaster, and I found out some things about the world and how things work.
The most valuable thing we have is time, and time does not stop no matter what happens time going. So like time we have to keep going. We have to keep growing and changing no matter what and that's not always easy. But while we fight change and growth, time is constantly ticking. Through the journey of growing, healing, and evolving there are so many paths, lessons obstacles and just everything you never imagined you must go through before you even begin to see your purpose and through all of that adulting you learn how to live. But the journey is what we don't speak about enough. The entire journey, like I wish somebody would've broken it down for me piece by piece, because I wasn't prepared for what came with

The Rebirth

Why don't we ever decide to change, until change is the only choice

We finally start realizing we have a problem when we can no longer rejoice

That's when we start asking questions, how'd I get here, why me

At this point in my life, I'm here and I'm in disbelief

Heavy is the head that wears the crown, that means if you want to be the boss, there's a price you must pay

You don't get a discount, and you have to work on your off day

Step one is accountability you must first, own your mistakes

That's why step one is always the hardest step to take

And I'll let you in on a secret, there's no warm up round

The moment you decide you want better, everything turns chaotic. If you make it past step one, you're a warrior, because you didn't turn around

And when you realize that you'll breathe a little better

But don't get to breathing too hard, as soon as you start breathing, that's when you get the real weather

That storm is called "bye ignorance" because that's what it wipes away

And that might sound like a good thing, but it's true what they say

Ignorance is bliss

A lot of things won't bother you until you realize it

When you find out blood does not always mean family, that might break you

And you might break again when you see you have no friends to turn to

And if death happens to creep up, baby strap in

Grief is a different kind of pain, it never goes away, and the feeling never ends

Your car might break down, you might even lose your job

Might gain a little weight, and begin to feel like a slob

In school you get a lesson then you get a test, in life you get a test, the lesson comes late

And until the lesson is learned you'll fail to elevate

Finding out the true colors of those around you is good, because
you need to separate

Everyone and everything doesn't deserve you but that's something
you must regulate

You need to realize who you are, what you deserve and you can
not negotiate

Don't get caught up in lust, sex is a very powerful thing

It's easy to lose yourself in the soul of another human being

If you fail to set your boundaries you'll consistently lose

Your growth is something you must choose

You have to be willing to fight for it

Now you know how things work so you can't just up and quit

I mean you can, but that's when life will become unfit

When you know better you must do better, or God will show you
why you should

He'll also open doors of opportunities for you when you believed
nothing and no one could

That's your reminder that you cannot stop, pause but you must restart

I know you failed, when you told your story, I heard that part

Failure is a break it is not the finish line

It means begin your task again, with more intelligence this time

Now you know a little more, seen a whole lot more and much more wise

Stop doubting yourself, act like you know who you are, and get back in route for that prize

Keep in mind all you've learned, apply pressure, be you

Now put yourself in position to do all the things you've always wanted to do

And when things start to come together remember to remain humble

That's how you survive when you're at war in the jungle

You needed to realize there are other lions around that need to eat

Everyone is not against you but no one wants to suffer defeat

So, you can play the victim and let times pass you by

Or you can use what you've learned to make better decisions next time

Eventually you get it right and everything will fall into place

If everything is not in place it's not yet the end of the race

Sometimes in order to grow you have to endure the storm

That's where your strength is formed

That's when you fight for everything you want, need and more

That is how you are reborn

That is where you learn your worth

Everything you go through is needed for your rebirth

#TruthBeTold

Once I figured out what I needed to do, I realized a lot of my faults and I saw some of my errors in more than a few situations and that made me take the time to give out a few

Necessary Apology

I apologize I failed to see you
I never wanted to hurt or mistreat you
I never meant to fight against you, or judge you like other people

I never intended to leave you hanging, I never wanted to see you
fall flat
I was never who you needed me to be, and I apologize for that

I'm sorry it took me so many years to see you like I do
I'm sorry I failed to appreciate all the storms you brought me
through

I'm sorry for any and every time you felt I gave you disrespect
I apologize for anytime my approach was incorrect

I was never the help that you deserved when you needed me to be
I wasted so much time, I'm sorry I blocked so many things

I'm sorry I failed to love and support you, I hate I failed to do that
I'm sorry I showed no compassion for the burdens I placed on your
back

I apologize I failed to see you because you've always deserved to
be seen
I apologize for being so aggressive I didn't realize I was so mean

I hate I failed to see you, I won't make that mistake again
Thank you for never turning your back on me, now we can
properly begin

#TruthBeTold

17

After I handled that as best I knew how I learned a great lesson, apologies don't mean shit. You can apologize until you're blue in the face, but that means nothing without changed behavior and while I was busy apologizing for the things I felt I may have done wrong to others, I failed to acknowledge the things I had done wrong to myself. Actually "I" had never even crossed my mind didn't even really know myself. One day I looked in the mirror and just asked

WHERE DO YOU EXIST?

Do you exist in your life, because I didn't know, I didn't.
And I couldn't give myself a real reason why I never lived up to
my potential
Why I never went hard for me, why I never gave my all
Why I never fought to climb whenever I bumped into a wall
Why I always waited to help myself
Why I never decided to do a little more, until I really had nothing
else left.
The only conclusion I could come up with was that I didn't love
me
I mean how could I truly
Love me
If I never fought for me
Never gave my all, I left so many things incomplete
So many relationships I cried about but never really put in any
work
I just believed if I was good, things would fall into place and I'd
never get hurt
I didn't exist in my life and I convinced myself that confidence
was key
That couldn't be further from the truth… confidence is strength,
and strength is what we use to cover up things
If we have the strength to suffer with a smile
You might convince yourself that things are ok… for a while
But eventually you'll get confident enough to really figure out
what's wrong
What's wrong with you, what do you really have going on
Why doesn't your pain matter to you?
Why don't you help yourself deal with your issues like you
encourage others to do?

Why do you think you'll always be ok?

What is it that makes you keep standing in your own way?

Do I really not love myself, I mean that's a harsh reality

Especially for me

But if I can't be honest with myself then who really deserves my honesty

I guess I don't love myself... so I don't know where I exist

That is something I had to fix

I blinded myself being soooo confident

I mean I truly believed nobody loved me, more than me... and I believed it

But when reality set in I couldn't see it

So, I couldn't truly receive it

That, I vowed to change and quick

If I don't love myself, there's no way I can demand it

I mean not genuinely

That's why I'm continuously

Wondering

Why so many crazy things keep happening to me

I had to start loving me

Allowing myself to grow, planting inside myself a love seed

I use to believe confidence was key

That's all changed, I now know its beauty

When you truly love yourself, you'll see how beautiful you are

There will be things you stop before they get too far

You won't allow certain things, they are simply beneath you

You'll allow yourself to grow and learn things you never knew

My beauty is love and that's where I exist

That's where I put it all on the line, that's where I take risks

Love is beautiful and for me that's beauty

And here's a little secret true beauty is the key.

#TruthBeTold

Realizing where I was verses where I wanted to be or better said, where I thought I would be, I just wondered how I was even able to maintain as long as I did, the way I was. How was I able to convince myself that everything was ok... it was my

<u>Confidence</u>

Confidence is key
However, confidence requires belief
Its belief that pushes you to keep going and succeed
When you believe you can, you will achieve
You must be confident you are strong when you feel you have no strength
When your mind is confident, your body will win
#TruthBeTold

When you have confidence you can damn near convince yourself of anything. Tell yourself something long enough you might actually start to believe it. If you seek to find the will to do anything in life big or small you must understand

It's in The Mind

Cultivate your mind to always envision optimism
Condition your ears to listen real clear, and free your mind from
egoism
Train your brain to align with Christ and let that adjust your
mannerism
Grooming yourself begins with the mind
Life teaches you this with time
All your answers lie with you inside
The key… is to cultivate your mind

#TruthBeTold

I began to train my mind to meet my aspirations, began to align myself with all the things I believed would get me where I wanted to go. I read some inspirational books, I listened and took notes from some powerful speakers, I felt empowered! I was ready to take on the world with my new attitude and a long list of

Expectations

Appreciate those that expect the best from you
But don't let other people's expectations control what you decide
to do
Expectations can break you if you fail to reach them
You can easily get caught up trying to redeem yourself and please
other people
Expectations can cause stagnation if you aren't careful how you
move
You can easily get stuck waiting around for what you believe is
obligated to you
That can cause you to waste good years
Bring you face to face with your biggest fears
Self-pity begins when expectations aren't met
Stress takes over and you fill your mind with regrets
When things don't go according to plan the beat down begins
Guilt, hate, and shame create a pain that can convince you life is
about to end
Usually when that happens it's something you can't see
Actually
Most times when you're declining, it's something you won't
believe
You'll isolate from family and friends
Feeling ashamed of the predicament you think you're stuck in
Take away expectations, bow your head and pray
Forgive yourself, for giving up on yourself and step out of your
own way
Take account for your mistakes, accept your flaws, and all your
sins
Take a breath, plan, and begin all your tasks again
People will expect things from you throughout your entire life
Just because it sounds good, and they know you, doesn't make
their words right
However, you should always listen when given advice
Although It may not be needed for the task at hand

Keep in mind there are many steps that complete a plan
We all know things don't always go as we expect
It's the unexpected things that give us the best affects
That's something I had to learn because I wanted to change and
grow
How to live my life knowing I failed to meet so many expectations
is something I didn't know
I had to force myself to move forward with so many disappointed
faces looking back at me
I wanted to meet all these expectations the world placed on me
I spent years doing that, but meeting other people's expectations
never gave me peace
And peace is the only thing I truly seek
I wanted the world to remove its expectations of me
I believed that would set me free
But actually
It was never the expectations that captivated me
It was my failure to expect the best from me
I had NO expectations for myself I believe in God, so I just knew
Somehow, I'd always make it through
But I never made a real list of things I should do
I hated every suggestion, no matter how true
Whenever they came my way
It was my lack of expectations for myself that made me turn away
If you have no expectations for yourself, your life is not your own
You're simply moving through life doing all that you're told
Then one day you'll look up and reality will set in on you
Its like wow I'm unhappy and I don't know what to do,
what's wrong, where to go
I have no one to talk to and I feel so alone
I didn't do what a few thought I would
Although I knew what I needed, and everyone knew I could
I have no excuse why I didn't do what I was expected to
I'm full of shame, grief and I feel like such a fool

27

I had no expectations for me, no plan, no next move
I didn't know how to express my feelings because it wasn't
expected of me to be confused
The world has a hard time accepting what it doesn't expect
That left me stagnate lost privately trying to deflect
Caught up in my emotions another thing I didn't expect
Other people's expectations can beat you down but yours will lift
you up
When you expect the best from yourself not even failure can get
you stuck
Make your own expectations and turn them to reality
Appreciate everyone that expects the best from you, that is your
family
Use their words as motivation
You'll need that to meet your own expectations

#TruthBeTold

The expectation phase of adulting is a rough one, it can sometimes feel like starting from scratch and while I was moving forward and accomplishing goals I'd set, something was still off. I was still mentally beating myself down for being so behind, for wasting so much time. I spent so much time dwelling on my short comings I began to feel ashamed and

Weak

We live our lives fighting anything that makes us feel weak
Weak is something we dare not be
Failure feels weak, to a mind that doesn't know.
You must fall if you wish to grow
That's how you learn the lessons you didn't know
Ironically when you run from the process your weaknesses show
You begin to slip down a slippery slope
If you believe you're weak you will eventually lose hope
You reveal your hand to all the wrong folks
People who've been waiting on you to choke
Finally see what holes to poke
Trying not to be weak
Is what makes you liable to yield or collapsed under pressure easily
That's the definition of weak playing out in your reality
Don't allow your weakness
To be your enemy's defense
If you always give away a valuable tool
That's a sure sign you'll always lose
Weak is temporary it leaves when you choose
To be strong and do whatever you have to do
In a nutshell if you don't want to be weak… change you
#TruthBeTold

So, I really started trying to change. (STILL TRYING, NOT YET DOING, DUH!) I wanted to be better I wanted to accomplish all my goals and I didn't want to feel WEAK! But that's how I felt, I didn't know how to shake it, and of course I didn't want to talk about it. I always felt talking was pointless, most people don't care, they just want to be informed, have a few facts to use to belittle you. Everyone is different, everyone has a different path, our differences are the best things about

Some of Us

Some of us were taught how to live
Others of us were showed how to survive

Some of us had to struggle for everything
Others were handed the tools to thrive

Some of us had to write our own story one chapter at a time
Others of us got written scripts, with tricks and codes between the lines

Some of us can't speak about certain things because we don't know how it feels
Others can speak on everything with stories that will give you chills

Some of us were taught to fight we must first self-protect
Others of us were taught its ok to be rude and disrespect

Some of us can't relate to others because we fail to realize
That we are all imperfect and that's what we can't deny

Some of us were nourished, spoiled, with love and affection
Others of us were deprived, raped of self-esteem childhood dreams, abused, and neglected

So, before you judge someone with a testimony you never knew
Stop and check yourself so that judgement doesn't becomes you
#TruthBeTold

We judge each other for things we've all experienced to some degree. It hurts to be judged. A lot of people kill themselves fighting judgement from others. Trying to fit into a world where nothing will ever be good enough, is a choking experience. Denying our hearts truest desires because they don't fit the bill. Forgetting what you love, to be what you hate, quickly became a way of life, and that baffled me. Life was changing, as I said it would, but I didn't let go of

Child Dreams

I believe we had life figured out back when we were kids
Before the world interfered and placed rules on the things we did
When we were young, innocent, and didn't have a care in the world
Before we were educated on life and our dreams were unfurled
The dreams we had as children are the dreams, we should have made come true
Those were the dreams that should've stayed in our view
The dreams that were our heart's truest desires
Then life came in
And new dream begins
While the old ones get lost in the wind
I wish life things
Didn't change child dreams
We should have never stopped living with belief
#TruthBeTold

Dwelling on the should've, would've, could'ves is how I again got stagnant I ran to old familiar places, ran into more than a few old faces and for a second... I was happy. Or so I thought I was. I was moving backwards comfortably and it didn't dawn on me that my atmosphere began to reveal the

Worst of Me

After years of living, my life taught me
Anyone who is content with the worst of me
Is the worst kind of person to have in my company

Let me please stop you, before you judge that statement you just heard
I have an explanation to precisely clarify my words
I know to many, that statement sounded so absurd
Like… no, true love will love you at your best and your worst
That's how you know it's real… that's the line we rehearse

Although, it is true
We all know its three sides to the truth
This side, that side, and then there's the truth

I gotta be careful loving someone that can love the worst of me
Love can make you content
Real quick
That's the very worst thing for me

If you can be content with the worst of me
That tells me you think the worst of me
So, the worst of me
Is the version of me
That you believe
To be the real me

That's an important part of how you treat me
That effects how interactions and conversations will flow between you
and me

If you think the worst of me
You'll have no problem disrespecting me
You'll feel no type of way about shortchanging me
In any aspect… physically, mentally, spiritually, sexually, and
emotionally
Never mind what I say, whatever I say, is wrong, or not what it should be

You don't see the tragedy
That currently
Is me
You'll always pull out the worst in me
And I don't need that company

The worst of me
Is exactly what its said to be
It's the bad inside the good of me
The feeling I keep in captivity
The anger that gets me caught up... occasionally

The worst of me
Is everything negative about me
I don't need anybody around me
Pulling out my negativity
Treating me negatively

If I allow that in my company
I'll also get content with the worst of me
Begin to speak to myself foolishly
Knowing I can do better but settling for mediocrity
Then I'll lose the desire to be the best of me
As a man thinketh, so is he
Slowly but surely, I'll become the worst of me

I don't wanna love someone that can be content loving the worst of me
Because the best of me
Is the only me,
I should be
If you fall in love with the worst of me
You won't be able to handle loving the best version of me
#TruthBeTold

Read: Genesis 39-41

<u>Section Two</u>

Realizing life has you in a choke hold causes the strongest of us to fold and fail. These are the times we yearn for answers, help and escape, we search for everything we don't have the answers for, some answers we find, some we don't, others simply lead to more questions.

So, there I was back in the mirror, except this time I was at rock bottom. I was in the mirror and looking back at me is what I saw and felt to be the worst of me. I was overwhelmed with disbelief I sunk so low I felt numb. Life was still going, so in that sunken place I had to keep going. I had to keep changing, keep growing, but I was dying inside. My soul felt weak, my confidence was low but time never stopped rolling, its Adulting. I was emotionally broken, and I wasn't speaking about it. I just cried to myself and begged for a

Time Out

I wish life had a pause button… so I could stop, think, and recollect… gather my thoughts and put my life into prospect… prospective… because my mind is going crazy… everything seems so hazy… my soul sometimes gets lazy… while I chase this dream I'm chasing. This dream that has become a nightmare… one of those nightmares you can't escape… the type of nightmare that makes you shake… traps you in your sleep so you can't awake… the type you feel throughout the next day… so much you must stop and pray it away. TIME OUT!

Now I'm stuck trying to figure out how the dream became a nightmare… how was that my reality and I wasn't aware… maybe I didn't care and sometimes when you don't care you aren't aware… of so many things that everyone else around you can see so clear. TIME OUT!

I need a break from reality… to properly regain my sanity… I'm going insane, losing my mind… I'm so sick of tears, and I hate when I cry… I don't know why, but I do… and that makes me cry harder if I tell the truth. TIME OUT!

I fell outta love with love, or maybe love fell outta love with me… that's actually… the biggest mystery… that exists to me… I'm searching and praying, but I really don't know what I'm looking for…feels like my body is sick and my soul can't find the cure… I pray for change… I've been living in hell so I'm praying for rain. TIME OUT

#TruthBeTold

But time doesn't stop, it doesn't take a break, or slight pause so neither could I. I needed to find my strength, but I couldn't be aggressive, I'm a woman and women shouldn't be too aggressive. I had to learn myself, find where my strength lies and release it, but not too aggressively, I'm a woman and women shouldn't be too aggressive. I needed to learn I didn't have to be aggressive. I'm a woman, women are born with a pussy, and

Pussy Can Not Be Weak

Pussy ain weak and at this point, I'm fed up
The disrespect has reached an all-time high
But today enough is enough

When you speak about the pussy, your speech should be spoken
with pride
Don't whisper the word pussy or slide it between your lines

Don't ever call me a pussy and think you're insulted me
The word pussy is sacred you might as well have called me queen

In the beginning it was the pussy that made the woman a
superhuman
We lay down
Then somehow
Nine months later we push out another human

How confusing for a man that can never empathize
With the strength of the pussy, he can only sympathize

Because he bursts up out the pussy with a dick between his thighs
So, in his eyes

Pussy pain is weak pain, pain his dick could never feel
And if the dick can't relate, well then it must not be real

Or at least not what you make it out to be
Just another exaggeration
Like every other explanation

"Just chill and take a seat
Better yet be more like me
The sympathy you seek

Is why I say you're weak"

Never mind all that smack
Listen to these facts

You were created inside the pussy
Bloomed from a seed planted inside the pussy
You were protected and fed inside the pussy

The pussy is power and represents nothing but strength
Pussy gives life, grooms, and grows a human within

Pussy can bleed for days without a cut or bruise
Pussy cleans itself removing its own residue

The pussy is elastic
Its flexibility feels fantastic

Pussy snatches souls and brings men to their knees
A world without pussy is a world so incomplete
The world is ruled by pussy so pussy can NOT be weak!

#TruthBeTold

I got my mojo back. I could feel my strength rebuilding. I was evolving. I am woman, hear me roar. After that I wanted to explore

Let's Talk About Sex

Its more than a physical act
Sex can take over your mind and control how you react
Sex is a beautiful thing when it's done right
Its spiritual, mental, physical, and great sex will have you up all night
Sex is how you make a baby that's why we must discuss it
Sexual mistakes hit our lives the roughest
Little girls and boys need to know how to protect their sex
Not because they're so young but because sex is so complex
You can give it away but sadly it can be taken
Teach a young child about sex so they're aware if ever in that situation
Let them know what they might hear, let them know what they might feel
Educate them so they can decipher what's wrong from what's real
Let's talk about an orgasm because so many don't know the feeling
Just having sex because it's a thing to do it not even fulfilling
Sex is a give and take situation ladies you should cum too
And if you don't know what that means, baby sex is not yet for you
Talk about sex, it also relieves stress, and that's what a lot of you need
Its not what you do its how you do it you just need to keep it clean
Let's talk about protection because STDs are real
Speak about sex and the possibilities because some of them kill
It's an adult activity and yes it feels good
It can also hurt if you aren't doing it as you should
Sex begins with foreplay and that's what a lot of you are missing
No licking, touching, sucking, rubbing, or kissing
Sex is personal and you're not supposed to let everyone in
I can go on and on about sex but that's where I'll end
#TruthBeTold

I didn't mention it earlier, but when I'm on an emotional roller coaster my sex life is at a low. When I'm too emotionally unstable, I'm not in the mood for sex, I don't desire it. I don't even think about it too much (but leave it to every man I've dated, I had other men during those times... I didn't) but once that roller coaster came to a stop, I began looking for a man to get

Inside My Walls

Before I let you inside my walls,
I must know exactly who you are

I must know your true intentions,
before we go too far

I need to know that you always plan to protect these walls
Before I let you in

I need to know you're worthy
before any fellatio begins

I must trust your capability
if you wish to cum inside my walls

you must be able to hold on
if these walls begin to shake, shiver, or fall

you have to meet my standards
if you desire to feel my walls split

Before I let you inside my walls
I must know for sure you're worth it
#TruthBeTold

Once I knew what I was looking for and what I needed to do I began that

Pillow Talk

Pillow talking in your ear
I want to whisper sweet things

Pillow talking in your ear wishing you nasty dreams

Pillow talking in your ear
Nibbling and kissing your ear lobe

Pillow talking in your ear somehow, I ended up on top

Pillow talking in your ear as my hips begin to rock

Pillow talking in your ear
Now you're talking too, and we don't want to stop

Pillow talking in your ear
I think the neighbors know your name

Pillow talking in your ear
I lost track of my nuts in this game

Pillow talking in your ear
He whispered back, now cum... and I came

Pillow talking in your ear Let's do that again

Pillow talking in your ear
I want this forever with my best friend

#TruthBeTold

After doing a lil talking, and a lil playing I found

<u>All Night & Day Recurring Ecstasy</u>

This is a love story that began
When a woman met a man
And honestly, I don't know when we met but I know that we did
Some years ago, way back when
We started off as strangers then evolved into friends
Time brought us so close he was so different than other men
We used to argue and disagree bicker and fight as friends
I didn't care what he did or how his free time was spent
We shared secrets talked for hours cried and vent
He was around to comfort me during all my traumatic events
And this man made me feel so safe I worried for people who
bothered me
His protection made me want to be a woman to him be soft gentle
and sweet

Baby… I'm talking true vulnerability

And keep in mind, this man I'm talking about, he was literally just
a friend
I never before looked his way, never thought he was cute, never
was he my type and THEN…

One day I looked at him… and felt something I could not
comprehend
I wanted to know him… the man inside the friend
And for me that was wild only because it was him
I was literally talking to myself like girl you tripping… and then
That lil feeling would come back again

And the type of friendship we had we keep it real
So, I was tripping yet again debating if I should tell him how I feel

I decided I was tripping, and I put those feelings on the shelf

52

There was no need to tell him, some things are better left with self

It had been a long time since I had my socks rocked, so I blamed it
on the hormones
You know when it's been a long time anybody is liable to rattle
your bones

So, time went on and I forgot that even happened
Things are back to normal, we're out hanging, like we do, eating
drinking and laughing
Then we locked eyes
And again, to my surprise
Those feelings began to rise
This time I've had a few drinks, so I'm beginning to wiggle and
rearrange my thighs
Ladies you know the vibes

I sipped my drink, looked in my cup
And swallowed quickly to shut myself up
Before I said the wrong thing
"Don't do it"
That's what my mind was saying
He looked at me and I know, he knew something was up
Looking dead in my face, he finally just said
"So, what's up, what you got going on"
I said Nothing drink went down wrong,

He knew that was a lie
He didn't say a word he just stared in my face and waited for my
reply

And you won't believe what I said next…
why did I tell this man I had a secret to tell him, but I didn't want
to tell him yet…

That was me just buying time hoping that these drinks will help
him forget

Who was I fooling I KNEW that wasn't gone fly
But I still said it and just went on with the night

We did some more bar hoping, we ended at a kickback
Nothing too deep just a lil group of friends getting together after
the club to talk smack
My friend and I are standing in the kitchen, talking and you know
what he said…
This man said
"So, you ready to tell me your lil secret?"

In my head I'm like dangggggg, why didn't you forget
I just brushed it off and said let's act like I never said that

This cool cat said ok, and conversation moved right on along
The night ended, we all left and went home

Next morning September 29th to be exact I can't remember the
year but that is the day
I'm pissed with myself for last night, I had too much to say
All bold and drunk

Then my phone received a text… it was my friend, just my luck

You wana know what he said?
Of course, ima tell you what he said…
He said

"I ain't even gone lie I know curiosity killed the cat… but I'm
curious to know what you were talking about last night"

At this point it was me vs myself and I was ready to fight

Now Niq why did you do this... that's what I asked myself
Why did you take those feelings off the shelf

My only response was well... I think he said it best... curiosity
killed the cat
No pun intended but he did just that

And that was another shock because I had never thought about him
sexually... until then

I told him my lil secret... and we talked about it for a minute
It was something that had never before crossed either of our minds
but now it did that, we both admitted

He asked me what made me feel that way
I said...
"It was your protection and love that made my feelings sway"

Gave me a desire to know a side of you I never knew
Feel you do things I never felt you do

And at this point we're both shocked, so you know what we did

We took our conversation from the phone to the bed

I can still hear him now
As he slid my thong down
"I ain even gone play with you" ... I said "please don't play with
me," then he took me to pound town

And I will tell you the truth he really shocked me

He gave me all night & day recurring ecstasy,

From the moment his skin touched mine I knew our friendship
would never be the same

It sometimes still shocks me that I love moaning his name
This man would say
"now cum"… and baby I came
He told me … "I got way too much love and respect for you, to not
blow your brains"
And that he did, I'm still tryna find the fragments
But the best part came after the sex, when our relationship evolved,
there wasn't a need for any adjustments
The vibe was the same
Nothing with our chemistry hindered or changed
Only now I wanted him in my skin
And I walked around daily dreaming of him again and again
He was now more than my friend
He was so much more
I felt like my body was made to cum for his… I felt him in my core
He tamed me again
As a man, not as my friend

This was a completely new way
Now…for him, I shut up and listen to what he had to say

That man rocked my world and turned me inside out
Sometimes I get caught up reminiscing and I forget what I'm
talking about

The craziest thing for me was, it was him, I couldn't wrap my
mind around that
We crossed the line… there was no going back

Hell, I didn't wanna go back, I wanted to evolve

Something erupted inside of me a mystery I had to solve

The sex was just a bonus to the love I had for this man
I went from loving him, to being in love with him so quickly I
couldn't understand

And that type of love is dangerous too dangerous for me

So, I had to apologize to my friend, and call me crazy but honey I
had to flee
My grandma Betty
Told me
To marry a man that loved me, more than I loved him

And I can tell by how things were happening
He wasn't about to be one of them

He gave me all night & day recurring ecstasy, I wanted him in my
skin
And that's exactly why he had to go back to being just my friend

I ain got time to play with him I had to move around
I wanted no parts in what he was consistently putting down
And he felt the same way I did…
We had to stop, before this started getting to our heads
We can't be doing that… at least that's what we said,

But in all actuality that was only how this love saga began
To Be Continued…

#TruthBeTold

When you get that type of loving it changes you, especially the first time. Its confusing, fascinating, and breathtaking. The mystery and thrill that lies within that love is what makes it so irresistible and completely unbearable both at the same time. That type of loving sometimes feels like

Fool Love

One of the many things love can do
Is make a fool of you…

Have you ever gone out of your way to avoid being made a fool
Just to one day discover the truth
And the harsh reality is despite your many efforts you were the
biggest and only fool
Now you're all emotional, feeling like joke is on you
Dissecting the entire situation
And every single conversation
To figure out how in the hell you got fooled
I mean you played your role, and paid your dues
You gave and loved like lovers do
Said forget the mess you had to go through
And truthfully, that's what made you a fool
All the things you chose to do
Despite the signs, vibes, or things you knew
Never mind the facts life revealed to you
You had a blind eye, even did things you said you'd never do
Nothing that happened stopped your pursuit
You were true to a feeling that felt true to you
So true you made yourself a fool
That's one of the many things love can do to you
#TruthBeTold

Remember in the beginning I told you time does not stop, while you're living, time is still never-ending. So again after trying all the wrong things I knew I wanted a

Lover And Friend

I want a lover and a friend
Wrapped up in one man
One that knows me
Loves the good, nurtures the bad, and tames the ugly side of me
Cares for me... shows it, the inside and out of me he adores
Protects me with no question, I'm his lioness bother me, he roars

I want a lover and a friend
Wrapped up in one man, that man requires a different me
Because he'll want some things from me
I want a man that wants the type of woman that I aim to be
A man that knows and accepts my past without judging me
I want a man that I will crave, every moment he's away from me
A wealthy man, wise and tough with amazing chemistry
One that trust me when I speak
And believes as I believe

I want a lover and a friend
Wrapped up in one man
one that understands my appetite mentally, and physically
And that man can't be any man I had to understand that literally
I asked myself so many questions, played so many things back in
my memory
I shake my head for the hurt I suffer regretfully
They say have no regrets if it happened it was best for me
All a part of my destiny
And when I meet that lover and friend
Wrapped up in one man
I'll smile at the past experiences I never have to experience again
#TruthBeTold

Moving forward to achieve what I want will require some new actions from me but I must trust the

Process

A few months ago, we broke up
and back then... I was a wreck

I was so full of emotions and that was something I didn't expect

We've broken up before,
many times, to be exact

but that time was different, that time, I knew I wasn't going back

for days... I'll even say weeks,
only you were on my mind

my thoughts were consumed with memories, moments shared
between you and I

my entire being was missing you
that was actually nothing new

but a few months ago, I chose a different avenue

I allowed myself to miss you
But that's all I allowed myself to do

I didn't allow the fact that I missed you
Cause me to step back into
A fantasy love rendezvous
Full of stress, bullshit, and things untrue
Undoing all the things I shouldn't undo

No, I allowed myself to miss you

Because that's a feeling I needed to get through
That missing you shit had to be subdued

There are better things I seek to accrue

A few months we broke up
And back then… I was a wreck

But I allowed myself to miss you and that had a different effect

Now I don't miss you,
Not even a little bit

Missing you was just a part of the process, and it was sooooooo
worth it
#TruthBeTold

For most of us solitude is scary, not for me. I love to be

Alone

I feel good when I'm alone
I work my best when I'm alone
Things get handled when I'm alone
I'm so free when I'm alone
No one judges me when I'm alone
I have no cares when I'm alone
I face my fears when I'm alone
If I step outside, I am alone
The language I speak, I speak alone
The words I write, I write alone
The battles I fight, I fight alone
When I right my wrongs, I do that alone
I cry real tears when I'm alone
I scream out loud no one hears when I'm alone
It sometimes gets lonely when I'm alone
When I feel unloved it hurts to be alone
When no one seems to care I hate to be alone
My mind cries wondering why am I alone
I think I work best when I'm alone
Things get handled when I'm alone
I'm so free when I'm alone
And when I die, I'll die alone
#TruthBeTold

Solitude is what I always need for

Elevation

Elevation requires separation
Separation means isolation
You need to be alone to figure out your proper placement

When you're really trying to elevate there's certain things you
can't do, certain places you can't go
Because when you're all in the mix somethings you just won't
know

At some point in life, you must decide it's time to elevate
It's a sad story when we wait
After years of giving desires and wants our chase
Then our lives begin to shake
Everything hurts and irritates
We see all the time we've waste
We're frightened at the challenge to escape
We see all we need to change
And you must change to elevate
It won't be easy there will be trials and tribulations
But don't let that stop you… proceed to elevation
#TruthBeTold

What we don't stress enough is how long and hard that elevation train ride is, like there's so much that occurs when you're growing and trying to be better, God tests you and teaches you so many lessons you have to have so much

Patience

Please practice patience
Please practice patience
Please practice patience

Yea that's a real tongue twister
But I had to say it three times, so you know I meant it.

Patience is a virtue, now that a real understatement
Your inability to be patient is why you're so irritated

Patience is a virtue that's a saying we all say
But do you really know what it means to be patient
Are you using it the right way
Most of us think to be patient means to wait

That's only half the definition
To be patient is to wait in peace,
PEACE that's the part, that's missing

If you aren't waiting in peace, you are not practicing patience
You're just simply waiting, and I call that being complacent

Please practice patience because patience calms you down
Patience keeps you cool when there's nothing but chaos going
down around

Please practice patience
Because it frees your mind
Gives you time to unwind
And find all the things you didn't know you needed to find

Please practice patience

#TruthBeTold

While everything is still moving forward you have to pay attention and use what you learned because that opportunity you need could happen at any moment and if it just so happens to be around the next corner

Would You Be

If you received what you wanted right now what would do

If the opportunity presented itself, would you be able to make your
dreams come true

Do you have all you need right now to get where you wana go

Why aren't you getting ready,
for those of you who's answer is no

So many of us want what we want, but we fail to go get it

We see what others are doing and we think we can do it too

Never mind what they had to go through

Or the plans they drew and pursued

If you stay ready you don't have to get ready that's a lil saying
people like to say

What's stopping you from getting ready,
stop standing in your own way

Get ready right now for whatever it is you want

So, when the opportunity presents itself all you must do is stunt

#TruthBeTold

Read: Genesis 42-44

<u>Section Three</u>

The truth is scary that's why so many of us spend our lives running
from it. But accepting the truth is the first step, once you know
what you must do, all you must do is move

You have to ask yourself questions like would you be ready, because its important you always stay prepared and be aware, aware of who you are, where you come from, and what you do, and don't have to your advantage. Its important to be mindful of this while Adulting. Most times

We Don't

We don't talk about suicide
We don't get to be depressed,

We don't believe in therapy sessions
Nor do we stop and rest,

We don't believe dreams can come true
unless we sell our souls,

We fail to inform our youth
of the power they hold,

We are taught to hate our skin
Persuaded and bribed to betray our kin
And somehow, we have the audacity to judge each other's sins

We don't know our true identity
Or desire to learn our history

And its hard to believe what you can do
When you don't know what you've come through

We don't teach the value of love and watching the company you keep
We no longer carry morals, and we forgot the meaning of loyalty
We don't get to feel redemption, our forgiveness does not redeem

Our mistakes follow us forever, they don't evaporate
We don't get to be kids when "kids will be kids" is the thing to say

We don't really know how to live
We had to first learn how to survive

So, we don't teach our youth to live

We show them how to stay alive

Encourage them to stay in line
So hopefully they won't lose their lives

We don't teach the power of unity
So, we fail to unify

We don't get to enjoy a life
We must battle to stay alive!

#TruthBeTold

Life is not fair... that's a harsh reality but the sooner you accept
that, the sooner you can use that knowledge to your advantage
dwelling in the unfairness of life can depress you, put you back in
a state you began running from in the first place. Time kept going
and I kept ending up.

Here Again

I never thought I'd be here again
Feeling the way, I feel again
You don't always do better when you know better
I knew the weather
Was hazy but I still chose to roam
Laying in the bed full of bad decisions I made all alone
And this time I'm unsure how to feel
I've been here before, so I know this feeling is real
This time I see the fault and I only have one question
I caught the blessing
But I never again want to have to be taught this lesson
Something must be different
I made some mistakes, but I was tripping back then
fighting demons, some who turned out to be friends
my road to recovery made me regret every sin
repent and fix what I broke back when I was drifting in the wind
I just want to be wealthy and see myself and my family win
And I never wanna end up here again

#TruthBeTold

When you get to this moment its your sign to stop before it gets worse. This is the "why me" stage. How did I get here, why did this happen to me, why me... why not you? It was you that needed to grow up and change. You want to prosper and be blessed. You want all the good, but you know before success comes

The Struggle

Everybody wants to skip the struggle
But you can't, the struggle is a part of the hustle

During the struggle you discover who's real and what's what
What doors to open, and which doors to shut

The thing about the struggle, that always pushes people away
Is it hurts... you gone go through some pain

The thing about pain, it teaches the best lessons
Sets you up to receive the best blessings

How you do one thing is how you do everything
When it hurts, you're determined to never go through that test again

Its not until you begin to struggle that you decide it's time to change
It's like that pain hits a trigger in your brain

That says, I can't do this no more
Its not until you begin to feel the struggle that, that tiny voice inside you
turns into a roar

You finally begin to focus on what you've been struggling for
Once you begin to focus, those blessings begin to soar

You're finally seeing clear and removing all the fickle
And once you begin to focus all the drama begins to dwindle

Because when you struggle, most times it hurts
That hurt
Forces you to get up, and put in the work
You're determined to put an end to the pain
That's why the struggle is a necessary part of the game
#TruthBeTold

When you know better you must do better. You go through the struggles to teach and show you what better really is. When you learn that you may want to share, but be mindful of the duties and responsibilities of

The Teacher

It takes courage to stand in front of a crowd and just speak
But it takes confidence, courage, faith, knowledge, money, and
purity to stand in front of a crowd and teach
If something is good for us, we're quick to object
If it means us no good, we listen closely before we reject
or accept
Knowledge must convince us
Foolishness only must interest us
We make it hard for the teacher in every form of teaching
Pay attention so you don't think I'm reaching
I said every form because teachers come in mysterious ways
But we judge them just the same
The teacher will forever first receive the blame
Get heavy hits, carry all the shame
Take the most lost, and feel the worst pain
But in the end
The teacher wins
And remember students the objective is to win in life,
It's not to be right
#TruthBeTold

call this phase the enlightenment phase because here is where you learn some harsh realities about yourself and you have to accept them so you can work them out, use what's needed and most importantly let go of

Bad Habits

No matter how in control you think you are of your bad habits
You will be judged because of your bad habits

The quantities you consume
Is what will speak for you
No matter how much you feel in tuned

Because there are many that lose control of their bad habits
Go insane
Deranged
Suffered pain
All because of their bad habits

So, you must be careful when you discover you have a bad habit
Be very careful when you discover you may have a bad habit
Don't waste your life engaging in too many bad habits
Especially if you can't control how you live with bad habits
#TruthBeTold

It takes 21 days to break a habit, every time I've decided to break a new habit with a 21day challenge, by day 10 I was

Screaming Inside My Head

Imagine walking down the street screaming inside your head
I mean not actually screaming because it must be done inside your
head

The desire to just AAAHHHH!!!

And maybe shed a tear or two
But the way life works I can't always stop, scream, or cry, even
when I desperately need to

Holding in emotions,
That eventually become screams that rage inside my head
Releasing pain and stress inside my head
Causing me pain and stress outside my head
Holding everything inside screaming inside my head

I can actually feel each scream
And if you've ever been overwhelmed you know exactly what I
mean

#TruthBeTold

Frustration can make you feel like you're losing your mind. When you're constantly irritated it may lead you to things to relieve you of that, reach out for help and grab hold of some

87

Pain Killers

Don't get too hooked on those pain killers
Don't go insane
Drugging your brain
With those pain killers

I know you may think you need a pain killer
Someway to ease your pain and hurt feelings
Here's a secret so very esoteric
The idea to kill your pain is a disease so endemic

Pain killing is a lie
Pain cannot die
You must learn to defeat pain regardless how it may arise

Train your brain to believe pain cannot beat you
Then pain will no longer be what defeats you
You'll no longer search for those pain killers
You beat pain without a killer, and you won't even shiver

#TruthBeTold

When you're sick and tired of being sick and tired, you're at your wick's end and you need to change there's only one thing that can truly move you to do what you must do

<u>You</u>

You must decide you're done
You must accept when that one you thought, really isn't the one

You must decide that you've had enough falderal
You must find a way to do the impossible when you don't know how at all

You must want what's right for you
You must be willing to do things you never thought you'd do

You must want change when change is what's best
And sometimes you must believe in yourself, YOU… no one else

#TruthBeTold

Once you wake yourself up you may look back on some things in amazement like wow

I Almost Let Myself Go
Pt 1: Lust

I almost let myself go, trying to hold on to you
And the thing that kills me is that you were absolutely okay
allowing me to.

No, "hey babe, while you're helping me fix me, don't forget about
you
Don't forget about the things you love, or dreams you wished
would come true

Don't forget about your smile, or stop laughing the way you do
And I don't mean those new jokes you laugh at now, cause they've
grown on you

Its like you didn't care what happened to me
When things got tough, you walked away from me
… that's the truth I didn't want to believe

I almost let myself go trying to hold on to you
I was lost in a daze, believing stories untrue
#TruthBeTold

Read: Genesis 45-46:27

<u>Section IV</u>
When you begin to move toward you purpose life will test you,
remember who you are, remember how far you've come, the plans
and changes you've made for you and stay the course

Getting motivated is great once you get back your motivation and reestablish your discipline its time to

<u>Try Again</u>

To fail does not mean you've reached the end
Failing is just an opportunity to begin your task again

Now you're more prepared, more wise, more informed
Now you can reach heights you never knew of before

Failure teaches you what not to do
Paths to avoid, doors and tunnels you shouldn't go through

If you have never failed, it's safe to say you've never taken any
real risk
Never really done any new things or found anything you felt was
"worth it"

You only fail why you neglect to try again
You will never fail if you continue to begin again
And again
And again

#TruthBeTold

Time never stops. Its important we keep up with time, but don't forget who you are, trying to keep up. In all aspects of life maintain your

Standards

First things first when it comes to standards, get some
Stop being ok being everywhere with everyone
People who don't have standards, hate those that do
They criticize every move you make
Every word you say
Simply because they can't get close to you
I don't do what you do, I don't go where you go
So, when you invite me places, most times my answer will be no
I don't think I'm better than anyone, but everyone doesn't deserve
to know me
I stand on that its not just something I speak
I don't change my mind because someone told me to
Anything I do its exactly what I wanted to do
I'm not willing to take a lost because of something you did
I don't mind standing all alone, I am not a little kid
Its not my job to comfort you
Or help you see things the way I do
I wish I didn't offend you
But I won't lose sleep because my actions or words lead me to
I'll never present myself as perfect
I also never had a doubt that I'm worth it
What is "it", absolutely everything
I'm a renaissance woman I indulge in many things
It's not what you do, it's how you do it
Sarcasm is my first language, in it, I'm very fluent
I said that to say I recognize slick comments and I catch shade
quick
When you have standards and live by them people are often
irritated
I can speak about cartoons, politics, superficial, scientific,
supernatural things
And all the stigmas they bring

I can talk to you about drugs, alcohol, and I will speak about God
I've never been like anyone else I've always been a little odd
The only thing I'm tired of doing is fighting the world to exist as
me
It's hard being unique
But I do it confidentially

#TruthBeTold

Living with purpose is amazing it gives you a sense of pride. When you're not easily assessable and you move to your own tune, things are revealed to you, that's why its beautiful when you find

I am untoufa

<u>Your Light</u>

If you've ever wondered why nothing seems to go right
Perhaps it's your inability to live within your light

You see God has a purpose for each and every life
Designated places,
Hidden tools in open spaces
On different levels and heights

He will always reveal your purpose to you
The question is when you realize yours, what will you do

Will you ignore the signs ahead of you
Choose to do what you know you shouldn't do
Or will you walk the rode paved just for you
It won't be easy, but it will mold you

It will also reveal some things to you
May even steal what you believe is important to you
But when you walk within your light you find peace
Wisdom, courage, and serenity

All that you seek is waiting for you somewhere within your light
So, open your eyes and see because it's time to get right

#TruthBeTold

Walking in your path you learn yourself on many levels, inside out and in that path you discover

What Is Black Beauty

Hello Black People, do you know your beauty
Can you see the diversity
Rooted so deeply
In your anatomy

Do you know that black beauty is a beauty unlike the rest?
Open the box
In which your mind has been locked
And see Black beauty is nothing short of complex

There is no one definition, there's no one specific kind
Black beauty is full of so many things you must expand your mind

Black beauty is power you must embrace it
Black beauty is conquering fears, trials, and tribulations
you have to face them

Black beauty is education never stop building your mind
Black beauty is understanding, especially those differences we try
to hide inside

Black beauty is history
Research and get to know your elders and ancestors they were
kings and Queens

Black beauty is support, you gotta give it and you need it
Black beauty is faith you gotta believe it to receive it

Black beauty went through slavery we cannot deny that
Stop running away from the pain in your past you gotta face that

Black beauty is your God given superpower all you must do is find
it

Black beauty is to be seen don't you ever try to hide it

Black Beauty is HARD!
And it really doesn't have to be
We make it so hard for black people to be black beautiful and free

Once upon a time if you wore red lipstick you were a slut
And if you wore white after Labor Day then... what?

Exactly we don't even really know what that means
but so many of us live by it or use to, that's how it seems

The world will try and convince you that black beauty is
something weak
Black beauty is just like any other beauty nothing really too deep

That, right there, is nothing but a lie I don't care what you heard
If it were true, so much emulation wouldn't occur

Why would anyone want to be something that's not absolutely
amazing
They wouldn't, that's why they deny its black beauty they're
imitating

Black beauty is a job, and it takes a lot of work
Black beauty comes with some heavy loads I'd be lying if I said it
never hurt

But black beauty is so full of love when you tap into what it really
is

Black beauty is the first thing you should teach little black children
when they are kids

A black child needs to know their beauty they need to know they
have power
They need to know that, to build their confidence so they know to
never cower

Black beauty is full of strength that's how we always pull through
Black beauty is recognizing the power inside of you

Teach a black child about their beauty because that's where they'll
find their peace
Because the secret I discovered is Black Beauty Is Key.

#TruthBeTold

Black beauty teaches you about

Energy

My energy is something I must protect
Because my energy keeps my attitude in check
Energy is neither lost nor destroyed, its simply transferred from
one party to the next
When you come around me, I need your energy at its best
This temper of mine whew… it's no joke
You think I'ma let you trigger that temper… sorry, nope
I'm very mindful of the company I keep and the energy they bring
The conversations they involve me in, and even the songs you sing
Bad energy can block your blessings, and nobody has time for that
Understand I don't care to be around you if you're energy is whack
This energy of mine is way too cool
If you're energy is full of negativity baby… I can't do you
I must protect my energy and that's all I have to say
If I'm not feeling your energy… I'ma gone on the other way
#TruthBeTold

Knowing how energy works, you're more aware of everything around and truly see no matter how much you stay to yourself people will still

Mind Your Business

Why do you care what he does in his free time
Why is that post she shared so heavy on your mind
Why are you so concerned how they wear their hair
Why are you pressed about other people's actions, why do you
even care
I understand the desire to know
But some go way too far, that's how problems get provoked
We are living in a time of meaningless opinions
Everyone wants to voice their thoughts about everything, when
most should just mind their business
What other people have going on is really none of your concern
The skeletons in their closet, you shouldn't care to learn
You won't always know what others are going through
Or why they choose to do the things they do
There are so many situations that would quickly cease and desist
If many of you would simply learn to mind your business

#TruthBeTold

Read: Genesis 46:28-47:28

<u>Section V</u>

There are many levels to the rebirth, it's important we do not get too comfortable. Change does not happen overnight faith and consistency are key that's how you continue to elevate when life feels as though you shouldn't

In my opinion, if you're doing it right, dealing with the world and trying to be a better you will always pull you closer to God

Let Me Explain

For years
I feared
To speak about my faith
I feared to you I'd sound insane
God works in mysterious ways
Those mysterious things sound crazy to explain
I'm not making this up God has shown up and out for me
That's why I want and urge you to believe
Get close to God and all your worldly desires will navigate
towards you
Live by his rules, believe his word is true
Watch him show up and out for you
Everything I ask God for he gives to me, exactly how I asked for it
Many times, I've received and realize I never wanted it
Whether I wanted it or not, I asked for it, so he gave it to me
That's the power of faith if only you believe
Many will say they don't know how to pray
I'm here to tell you that's okay
There's no right or wrong way to say
"God, I need you," that's the very best prayer to pray
You see he knows what you need, he just needed you to come to
him
When you realize you need God he'll show up and quickly you'll
begin to win
But here's the other side that many fail to receive
If you believe in your faith, you will give generously
Whatever you must give and that's not always easy
Actually, most times it's very hard and always complicated
That's how you show your faith, it's a give and take situation
You must have faith that all things that are happening or happened
for your good, somehow you needed what you got
That's how you keep moving forward when all you wana do is stop

Being faithful is hard, the more you believe, the harder it gets
As your faith grows stronger you understand its always worth it
I've gone through some things, but I know God was molding me
Opening my eyes
Expanding my mind
And providing me
Tremendous opportunities
But before he blessed me
He tested me
Just to be sure I was prepared for whatever I asked for in prayer
These days I'm very particular about what words I put out into the
atmosphere
I know the power of words and I answer to a big God who always
has his eyes on me
I can't worry about humans and the things they say or believe
I can't allow my desire to feel good in the moment block me from
feeling good for life
I'm tested and if I fail, I'm tested until I get it right
I'm not perfect but I don't play with or about my faith
I've personally witnessed God work in mysterious ways
I know he will do just as his word said he will
That's why I choose his word, most times, regardless how I feel
It was my faith that gave me peace
In moments when I should have felt defeat
Those moments amazed no one more than they amazed me
How can I feel so complete in the middle of catastrophe
How is my head holding high when my shoulders feel so heavy
It's the God in me
Whenever I come face to face with controversy
I turn to God, but he knew the moment was coming
He knew I'd be here, he prepared me so there's no running
There I can choose to trust him and walk through the flame

I couldn't let fear defeat me and remain the same
This time I'll try and trust his word and if it works out for me, I'll
know God is real
That's how it begins and now today I know the deal

I speak things into my life, and they occur
I speak to my family and friends and I'm careful with my words
I had to change my life because I know God and I know how he
works
I'm not willing to allow a lack of faith to ruin what I've witnessed
occur
I don't always do as I could
But every time I don't God shows me why I should
And that all may sound crazy to you
I can't make this up it's all true
I would be dead and gone If I were living for me
You don't have to trust my word, try God yourself and believe
Try God and you will receive

#TruthBeTold

One thing I realized and keep in mind daily after experiencing some of the things I have, my parents were growing and

<u>Human Like You</u>

The bible says honor thy mother, thy father so that's what we must
do
Forgive your parents for being human and making mistakes just
like you

Parenting is a journey parents must slowly navigate themselves
through
I wana talk to you about your parents, that chastise the things you
do

They're trying to prevent you from going through
Some of the same things they went through

They see themselves in their child
And they remember what they did back when they were wild

But now they know what those actions will cause
And they refuse to sit back and watch you fall

They only want the best for you
Parenting doesn't come with a manual, in the beginning they don't
know what to do

They don't even yet know you
What you'll do
Who you'll grow into
When to push verses when to pull you

But parents please don't push too hard because you can push your
child away
Everyone gets tired of fighting no one, not even your child wants
to fight with you everyday

Understand being "the parent" doesn't mean you're always right
Sometimes a simple apology can fix the broken if only you try

Don't feel as though your child must always come to you
What happens when they're beaten and broken, and they choose
not to
You can lose years, memories, you can even lose a life, either one
of you

Contrary to popular belief mommy and daddy issues are real
When you grow up without a parent, everyday that's something
you'll feel

Don't let that make you bitter, their absence may have been best
Who knows who you may have turned out to be, had they never
left

If they happen to return, please receive them
Honestly, you're never too old to need them
#TruthBeTold

Maturing is what pulls you through everyday. In the growing process you have to have a lot of understanding. I came to find that more and more I grow through God. I've never been more mature, felt more aware than I do now and I can truly say

This Is Peace

A faithful life is not an easy life
But a faithful life is a peaceful life
You and I are so unworthy and both sinners alike
But that doesn't matter to God he never leaves our side
Through my relationship with God, I am finding peace
He teaches, grooms, and sometimes even beats
But that's my testimony
God has brought me through everything
Everyday I'm growing, he's constantly teaching me
No day is perfect, and neither am I
I'm a sinner no different from you and he never leaves my side
I want the world to love God but to more so believe
Only if you believe can receive
The love and security that has been privileged to me
Through my relationship with God, I am finding peace
I'm learning to love the world as he loves me
And I'll let you in on a secret, I've never been this happy
I'm thankful Jesus died for my sins and privileged this life for me
Always first make God the thing you seek
And I promise you'll find peace
#TruthBeTold

Finding peace is a beautiful thing and I wanted to share that, but I wanted to share it correctly with the right one, but what exactly is the right one, I mean when it comes to a man

What Do I Know?

What do I know about a man
Not as much as I thought, that's for sure

And the older I get the more I understand
Some things only make sense once you've matured

As a woman I know how it feels to be near
And dear
To the heart of a man

As far as what's going on, on the inside, tell you about that
Only a man can

I wana get to know men
But there's only one man with whom
The rest of my life I wanna spend

That is why when it comes to this topic
I have so many questions

I thought I had so many answers and yet
I continue to run into the same dilemma over and over again

I thought it was all in my head
Like Nelly said

But then reality set in
And I realized… this dilemma existed inside
And outside
My mind

But the crazy thing was somehow, some way
A man can be trapped so deeply inside my mind

Yet the key
To unlock me
He can't seem to find

If I tell him no means yes sometimes
He can't understand why

That's another thing I realized

The mind of a man is so complex to break it down so a woman can
Understand...

Only a man can

I can tell you how it feels to be in the presence
Of true masculinity

And I can tell you how what I see
Makes things inside me ting

Thinking about...
That thing

I'll stop before I begin to daydream
About some things

Any woman ever been properly handled by a real man
Sista
You know what I mean

Back on topic I can tell you what I think is going on
Inside his mind

Based on past situations I've encountered
Over time

But I can't explain why men are so irritated

I mean I get that life sometimes
Is very frustrating

But men don't have cramps
Or must deal with hoe stamps

They aren't labeled weak
They are the face of masculinity

They don't carry a breed

They just shoot the sperm
That impregnate the seed

And they really don't have to stick around after that

That's why so many flee
Easily

Go on living their lives oblivious
And peacefully

Leaving behind a generation that blooms and grows
So dysfunctionally

122

And if they try and come back
No one cuts them any slack

I feel as though no one should

I mean you walked out on your responsibilities
And no one knew you would

So don't expect an easy path even if they could

It's a man's world we live in
Everything is built to benefit a man

To tell you why a man truly loses things and snaps
Only a man can

It's been years
I've cried many tears

Trying to find answers
That still wouldn't make things clear

And sometimes the answers to those questions
Reveal our biggest fears

Why do men do what they do
Why are they the way they are

Some men have more discipline
Some men have more to live for

Some men were given their home, foundations, rules, and tools
Other had to build their own doors

Women have the same plight
But it's a different kind of fight

I don't mind if you disagree
But women receive a lot more sympathy

There are not many souls in the world
That don't care
To share

What they can when they see a woman in need

Especially one with a baby

And I'm not making any excuses
I'm just speaking on what I know
About a man

But to say if I'm right or wrong
Truly
Only a man can
#TruthBeTold

Read: Genesis 47:29-50

Section VI

Acceptance may be one of the hardest steps to walk. Having to be
ok with things you cannot change or truths you never wanted to
live is HARD. But that's life, that's the main fact they never
mention about the rebirth

One thing I do know, is when it comes to a

Black Man

Blackman

Every day I pray for you
I pray you're fully equipped for whatever life takes you through
The world is tough and against you, the day you escape the womb

Blackman,

You're depicted as a threat first day breathing air on earth
Before you open your eyes, you're feared, so many know you're worth

Blackman,

You are never unarmed, you were born with a fully loaded pistol
A melanin shooting missile
That shoots the most powerful seed
A seed that carries his breed
Regardless to the womb he selects

Blackman,

You are born so powerful, more powerful than the rest
In fact
That is the exact
Reason you are depicted as a threat

Blackman,

Marry a black woman and make beautiful black babies
Stick around and raise those babies to be gentlemen and young
ladies

Blackman,

Don't fall apart if life begins to tear you down
It's okay to cry, you don't always have to smile

Blackman,

Don't rush your life, you won't miss what's meant for you

Blackman

You are a king, time to do what kings do

#TruthBeTold

And I hope you haven't forgotten that still while you're growing, finding peace, and realizing where you want to be life is still life-ing. Ups and downs are still occurring. One thing we cant prevent is death. It comes for us all, whether we're ready or not that's why we must

Learn How to Grieve

I urge you to understand death and allow yourself to grieve
Living with the hurt of death while trying not to grieve makes it so
easy to choke and so hard to breathe

Death may not seem fair to you
But it is something you must learn to get through
Death is a mandatory part of life
Some things and people must die for things to continue or turn out
right

All things will eventually come to an end
You must learn and understand death, so you don't break, its ok to
bend
Don't be afraid to cry, and don't hesitate to shed a tear
Grieve for your loved ones, never forget they were here
Grieve every time you need to, grieve anywhere

Sometimes in grief we pray for time, more time to love and spend
Those are sometimes selfish prayers, we pray to hold on to our kin
What we fail to realize or understand is real peace sometimes,
comes in the end

They pray for strength to hold on for me and you
We pray for time to watch them struggle through

Death is not easy to accept that's why we must grieve
Grief has the power to take over anyone, that you must believe

It has a way of stealing you happy while raping your entire soul
One day you look up so lost in a daze in a world so cold
You can't breathe from holding back tears
Holding back your chance to properly heal
I pray you find strength to cry, scream, shake, and shiver

130

Whatever you need to be delivered

Grief feels like a choke hold
Free your mind and your soul
Pray for strength and take control

Don't live a life of misery
Trying not to grieve
Trying to seem happy when you're dying inside, causes your true
happiness to leave

Learn how to grieve so all that can cease
You won't ever fully heal but you can find peace.
#TruthBeTold

Grief is never-ending, the only way I know how to navigate my way through it is

Faith Travel
11/6/20 6:28am

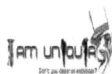

God is the key to whatever you may be going through
Get closer to him and all your worldly desires will navigate
towards you
It's a blessing to know God and to have this faith
Faith travel
Is safe travel
Directions are received when you pray

Going to church don't make you saved, but saved people go to
church
There you commune with others,
Receive a message,
Learn a lesson,
And begin to heal where you hurt

I asked God to heal me, help me to be a better me
I had no idea the places he'd take me on this journey
One thing I know for sure, God is real
Every time I ask a question, the answer is revealed

When you ask God to make you better, the devil will come to
destroy and kill
Those are the moments life is so hectic we feel we can't deal
It's hard to stay faithful when life has you turning and tossing

But you are closest to the light when the tunnel gets its darkest
Get closer to God and he will heal you
Faith travel
Is safe travel
Prayer guides, and God never leaves you!
#TruthBeTold

The rebirth journey is full, its truly an experience and if we talked about it more we'd make it a little less hard, I always wondered

Why Don't We Tell It All

When we tell our glory story why do we hide the shame
Why do we elude the embarrassment we endured and the things
that made us change
Why don't we share our experiences exactly as they occurred
Tell each other the holes we fell in the location to exactly where
they were
The answer is actually simple and sad from what I've observed
Many are envious that another may succeed, so they don't share
the word
Fear that another pass you
After all you've been through
Is the mindset that enables a community
I won't share because if you happen to move ahead of me
I'm unsure what it will do to me
So, I won't share with you my secrets to prosperity
And if things just so happen to become your discovery
I'll make it my business to hinder your recovery
I can not allow you to get ahead of me
And in the mind of one, that thinks as such
Stupidity is what they don't believe they have much
Somewhere along the line people have become convinced
That lighting one candle with another causes the other one to dim
Thats why we don't tell it all we don't want to lose
But what we need to know is sharing information is important to
do
Its actually an important tool
Together people can reach heights they never even knew
Harriet Tubman was not the best, because she ran away
She was the best because she made a way
And went back to show others how to do the same
#TruthBeTold

135

Many people in life have struggles we may never know about and growth teaches you to be kind, because of this we are all born different. Our differences make us beautiful

Disable Me

Imagine one day you woke up and you had a disability
Maybe you can't move, comprehend, or you're struggling to speak
I pray the world won't look at you and criticize what they see
I pray you love yourself abundantly
And don't believe those that try and make you feel weak
What if you struggled to learn new things because your brain was
not developed the same
And sometimes you fail to recognize something as simple as your
own name
What if you're focus doesn't focus as everyone else's does
What if you lost your mind and threw a tantrum just because for
the first time you heard a bee buzz
What if your body began to snap out only because you're irritated
What if every time you open your eyes suicide was contemplated
How would you feel if you couldn't control yourself
How would you hurt
if your body didn't work
or you didn't function like everyone else
What would you think of you
If you knew
Sometimes you weren't you
And in those moments, you said and did things you normally
wouldn't say or do
You see disabilities and mental Illnesses are real
Its best we educate ourselves so when we encounter people and
situations you know how to deal
It is unfair to them that they were born disable
It is 10 time more unfair that they must deal with those of you, that
are hateful
Really and truly ungrateful

Because you were born capable
To be a blessing to those that need just a little bit more love, a little
bit more time, and a whole lot more patience

The sweetest people in the world… hate, they should never have to
face it
Lord disable me if I ever show hate to someone in need
Especially some who is sick or has a disability
#TruthBeTold

Treating people how you want to be treated is a life tool. It'll get you very far in life. How you treat people matters, who you are and what you do matters. We were all called to be different. People achieve different goals that's why its important to have a

<u>Strategy</u>

I live my life strategically
I'm a child of God and he
Chose me

I use my words to paint pictures, I'm not good at expressing
myself

Not to strangers at least
I must feel absolutely
Positively
And totally

Comfortable in your space
Know you so well I'm aware what's okay
And what's not okay
For me to say

That's a hard way to be
Maybe that's how it seems
But to me…
Its strategy

I must live my life strategically
I'm a child of God and he
Ordained me
What you call hiding I call respect
I'm not going around the parentals drugged up, geeked up, cussing
and that's just that
I don't promote my demons I know I'll have to pay for all my sins
My misery

Doesn't like company
I want all my people to win

I'm not trying to pull a soul
In a hole
When I fall in

That's when God is trying to tell me something
When I need a moment to replan my strategy

I must live my life strategically
I'm a child of God and pleasing him is what's important to me
#TruthBeTold

Organizing your life to get where you want is not being fake, its being wise. You have to make changes, remove yourself from spaces and discipline like never before, that's only

If You Want It

If you are silent about your pain, your enemy will kill you and tell everyone you loved it... and although that be a lie
That's what we'd have to believe because you never said otherwise

So, if you truly want to be heard first thing you must do is speak up
If ever you feel disrespected, you need to stop and clear some things up

You don't have to be abrupt you can keep it cute
And still get your point clear to through

If you truly want things to change, there are some things you must change
Its time everything be moved and rearranged

There will be things you no longer can allow
To grow, you gotta learn how to shut things down

Don't get in the habit of allowing people to mistreat you because that's a hard habit to break
And the reality that someone you loved was mistreating you, that's a hard reality to face

And the fact that you allowed it to go on so long that's the biggest slap
Shut it down, shut it down... you don't wanna feel that

Shut down the desire to be accepted because everybody won't accept you
Instead build your credentials if push does shove all the world can do is respect you

143

Don't get caught up in the drama misery loves company
I don't know about you, but I don't need the bull disrupting me

Shut down that need to be right, everyone will not see things your way
And that's no reason for you to find hateful things to say

Speak up about your problems so we can shut down all the hate
And make some changes that positively affect our fate
#TruthBeTold

When you decide you want better and you're putting forth the effort to be better discipline yourself to keep going and growing, everyday will be a new day each and everyday

Remember to Win

Yes. you were right, but did you win
That's the real question
It's better to win than to be right, that's a real lesson

A lot of times we are right, but we still lose
But we love to be right and that's how we play the fool
Everyone must agree and say yes to all we ask
But did you know to win in life is the real task

We've all seen millions of men
Lose years for crimes they didn't commit
They were absolutely right when they said they were innocent
But they still did the time
Because in the real world we can't rewind
That's just a lost you must take it on the chin
I don't care to be right if I win

That lesson will save you so many arguments
With ease
You breathe
Sit and simply say
Okay
You got it.

To many, that seems weak
To others its seen as defeat
But to me it's a win
That's how you save yourself from pointless debates that never end

If ever you loan someone some money and they fail to pay you
back
Don't trip
That's their slip

Moving forward they can never again ask you for jack

For just a little bit of change you are free of a leech
You save yourself those moments of frustration when you have to
ask "when you gone pay me"
No, I'll take the win and leave
Let them continue avoiding me
That's where I am… maturity

It takes maturity to understand that its more important to win than
it is to be right
That's the objective… to win in life
#TruthBeTold

Ladies and gentlemen thanks for reading comeback soon to the Pluumtree #TruthBeTold

About The Author

Uniquia Manigault, one of the world's leading and creative poets, has been teaching and coaching performing arts for many years. Uniquia is Founder/CEO of I Am Uniquia Co LLC and author, professional actress, model, poet, host, entertainer, comedian, beauty advisor and fashion show presenter. She's also the founder of Black Girl Beauty Performing Arts School. At her school she's a coach for acting, modeling, poetry and hair braiding, professional development, leadership and entrepreneurship for youth ages 5 – 18. She also teaches adult model aerobics. Uniquia is a motivational speaker and teacher and can be booked for future engagements.

To contact Uniquia write:

Email: info@iamuniquia.com
Or call: 470-241-6941
Internet address: www.iamuniquia.com
www.blackgirlbeauty.org

Please subscribe to our newsletter and email your testimony/review or help received from this book when you contact.

You may follow Uniquia at:
LINKEDIN: Uniquia Manigault
FB: Black Girl Beauty Performing Arts School @Uniquia Manigault
IG: BlackGirlBeautyBGB
Twitter: Uniquia Manigault

Words From The Author

Life is an unwritten journey. Don't be afraid to explore it. Don't be afraid to be you, and don't be afraid to make mistakes. Often in life we miss out on the greatest things because of fear. Fear of what might happen; Fear of what might not happen: and Fear of the possibilities. Don't let fear hold you back, because fear will be your only regret. With faith anything is possible. Fear has no dwelling where faith is instilled, because you can do all things through Christ who strengths you. God has no respecter person and you've never fallen so far that you can no longer stand. We aren't promised an easy life, but we're promised to never have to journey alone. He'll never leave us nor forsake us. In the end, all things will be ok; and if they're not it's not yet the end. Keep the faith and never quit! Everything will happen in due time, exactly when it's supposed to.
#TruthBeTold.

Thank you for reading
Uniquia Manigault

www.ingramcontent.com/pod-product-compliance
Lightning Source LLC
Chambersburg PA
CBHW060752100426
42813CB00004B/783